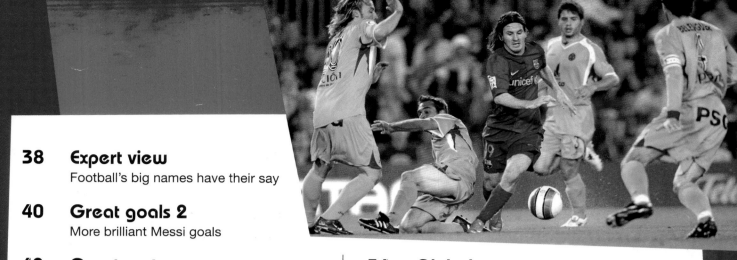

KT-378-045

INTRODUCTION

From the streets of Argentina to becoming the best player on the planet, the story of Lionel Messi is a footballing fairytale.

Messi's story proves that it doesn't matter how big or strong you are, or how rich your parents are, or where you were born. Anything is possible if you are good enough and you work hard enough.

Messi has always had a special talent. That was obvious from an early age when he grabbed every chance he could to improve his skills, and soon the older boys were struggling to get the ball off him.

That has been the story all the way through Messi's life as helpless defenders struggle to stop him. When Messi is at his best, nobody can stop him. The number of goals he has scored and trophies he has won prove that.

By the end of the 2018/19 season the little magician had netted more Spanish league goals (419) than other player in history. His incredible exploits brought him 10 La Liga winner's medals, four Champions League triumphs and three FIFA Club World Cup crowns.

Even a medical problem which stopped him from growing properly as a child has not held Messi back. Barcelona were so keen to sign him that they paid for the injections which helped him grow and they have been rewarded in style.

It is why Messi will always be grateful to his club. Barcelona were the ones that helped turn his dream into reality as he made Spain his new home. The move to Europe could not have worked out much better. Football may never be lucky enough to see another player quite like Messi. He has been a true legend of the sport for more than 15 years.

Perfect role model

The success has not gone to his head either. Despite everything he has won, Messi remains modest about how good he is. It is not just his skill that is a shining example to everyone. His behaviour and his attitude make Messi the perfect role model.

Football may never see another player quite like the Argeninean, but the good news is he is far from finished despite dominating the game for so long. He may have turned 32 in the summer of 2019 and, after scoring an incredible 51 goals for Barcelona in 2018/19, he's showing no signs at all of losin any of his amazing powers.

He is a true football superstar.

Lionel Messi played in his fifth Copa América for Argentina in 2019, and was captain in 2015, 2016 and 2019.

LIONEL MESSI
THE ULTIMATE FAN BOOK

FOURTH EDITION

Mike Perez

WELBECK

CONTENTS

Messi hails the Nou Camp faithful on the eve of the new season in August 2019.

EARLY YEARS

The little boy who became the world's greatest footballer was born in a modest area and needed medicine to help him grow. When Barcelona paid for his treatment, his future was sealed...

Lionel Andres Messi was born on June 24, 1987 in Rosario, Argentina. It was a time when Diego Maradona was the big superstar in the South American country. Around one year before Messi was born, Maradona had been captain of the national team that won the World Cup in Mexico.

He possessed many of the same skills as Messi has now and he was able to slalom past defenders like they weren't there. Many believed he was the greatest player there had ever been, along with Pele of Brazil.

Just 12 months after Maradona inspired Argentina's success at Mexico '86, a new star was born.

Messi was the youngest of three brothers for parents Jorge, a steel factory worker, and Celia, a cleaner, while he also has a younger sister.

He lived in what he describes as "a nice, ordinary house" that his family still own. Having received his first ball when he was around four years old, he started playing with his older brothers and cousins.

The house did not have a garden, so Messi would enjoy kickabouts in the street outside his home in the run-down area in which they lived. It was not long before he joined neighbourhood side Grandoli, where father Jorge was involved in the coaching and most of

his family played at different levels. It was already clear his son was a very special talent as other boys struggled to get the ball off him.

A shy and humble Messi kicked a ball at every opportunity outside the school classroom. At the age of eight, he went on to join the youth system of local professional side Newell's Old Boys. It was the club that Maradona had not long left as his own career was drawing to an end.

Expensive injections

However, just as obvious as his outstanding ability, it was becoming ever more apparent that Messi was smaller than most other boys. Around a year or so after joining Newell's Old Boys the doctors discovered he had a restrictive growth hormone deficiency, meaning he was not growing as much as he should.

The expensive injections to help him grow were paid for at first but all that would change later. Messi's family were left with huge costs to pay for his continued treatment. Newell's Old Boys were unable to afford the bill and Argentina giants River Plate – a big club who were watching Messi – did not want to pay either.

In 2000, when he was 13 years old, Barcelona came into Messi's life to start a journey that would take him to the very top of the game. He was invited to Spain

"It wasn't difficult for me to move to Barcelona because I knew I had to. I needed money for my medicine to help me grow and Barcelona were the only club that offered."

Little Lionel feels the cold in a paddling pool with his two older brothers.

for a 15-day trial and very quickly made an impression on Barca technical director Carles Rexach. He had nothing else to use so, incredibly, he agreed to sign Messi and pay for his medical bills in a contract that was written out on a paper napkin!

Messi and his father returned to Argentina where the rest of the family started packing their bags to leave South America for Barcelona, just as Maradona had done himself back in 1982.

"It wasn't difficult for me to move to Barcelona because I knew I had to," Messi said. "I needed money for my medicine to help me grow and Barcelona were the only club that offered. So as soon as they did, I knew I had to go."

The little four-year-old Messi (standing, second right) was soon showing off his skills with local children's team Grandoli in his home city of Rosario. Below, he is second right in the front row two years later.

SUPER-CAMPEONA CAT. 87 "A"

MAKING OF A GENIUS

ATTITUDE
Often seen with a smile on his face and humble about his record-breaking achievements, Messi simply loves playing football. And he nearly always does so in the right way – with 100 per cent commitment, honesty and loyalty.

RESPONSIBILITY
Being the leading player on the planet is a heavy burden to carry, but it does not seem to affect Messi, who rarely produces anything less than his world-class best week in, week out.

LOW CENTRE OF GRAVITY
Perfect example of how smaller players can use their size to their advantage. With superb balance and great lower-body strength, Messi is able to ride tackles, weave his way through the smallest of gaps and change direction in a flash to leave opponents bamboozled.

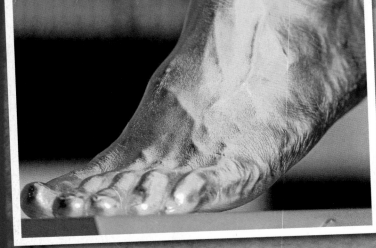

THE WIZARD'S WAND
It often looks as if the ball is glued to Messi's left foot, such is the brilliance of dribbling and control. It is also a deadly weapon when it comes to shooting. Messi is equally capable of smashing home a screamer from long range as he is delicately chipping a helpless goalkeeper. A gold cast of Messi's left foot went on sale in Tokyo for more than £3.4 million.

INTELLIGENCE

Messi's razor-sharp brain, combined with his natural talent and instinct, make him the ultimate attacking machine. He is ultra-cool when in goalscoring positions, rarely wasting any opportunity to find the back of the net, while he is also just as good at creating goals for team-mates with his awesome passing.

DETERMINATION

Messi was told he would not make it as a professional footballer as a youngster, but never gave up his dreams and has proved the doubters and critics wrong in spectacular fashion.

PACE

He is deceptively quick and his tremendous acceleration from the second he picks up the ball allows him to speed past defenders before they have a chance to react. Messi has admitted that being smaller has forced him to become faster, and there are few who can keep up with him when he is in full flight.

SPANISH ADVENTURE

Although small in stature, Messi did not take long to make a big impression at Barcelona after moving to Spain with his family.

Starting at the Spanish club's famous La Masia training academy – a sort of Hogwarts for talented young footballers – Messi's raw natural ability was clear to see.

However, it was not all plain sailing for the quiet and shy young South American in his first few years in Europe.

Messi had all the normal problems of trying to adapt to a new life in a new country. He suffered an ankle injury in his first season too, which ruled him out for a while. A delay in getting registered properly also delayed him being able to play competitive matches for Barcelona.

Swift and spectacular

He finally received his playing licence from the Catalan Football Federation on March 6, 2001, and Barcelona wasted no time in giving him a chance to show what he could do, handing him his debut with the boys' team just 24 hours later. Wearing the number nine shirt, those watching that day in the match against

Amposta would have seen something that would become as regular as clockwork in the years that followed – a Messi goal and a Barcelona win.

Messi's rise after that was swift and spectacular. As he grew in size and improved his stamina, Messi was increasingly able to show what he could do. He made his way up through the various youth ranks at Barcelona in lightning-quick fashion as he quickly proved himself good enough for the level above.

Josep Boada, one of Messi's first coaches at Barca, recalled: "He had an extra gear. If the top gear was fifth, he could find a sixth, and that meant at some times he was unstoppable."

Messi was initially played wide out left in the Barcelona youth teams, but he kept drifting into the middle. He was looking to become a playmaker who controlled matches and scored goals, like his idol Diego Maradona.

It was a playing style Barcelona fans have now become well accustomed to. After his rapid progress through Barcelona's youth teams on the back of

Messi (front, second left) lines up with the Barcelona youth team. Also in the picture are Gerard Pique (back, fifth left) and Cesc Fabregas (back, third right) who would go on to become senior colleagues.

"He was small and skinny, but when he had the ball at his feet he had a tremendously competitive spirit."

an avalanche of goals, Messi soon found himself representing the club at Under-19 level despite still being much younger.

Pere Gratacos, who was in charge of Barcelona's B side between 2003 and 2005, said of the young Messi: "He was an extraordinary player. He did things with ease, making difficult things look easy, and he did this regularly, it wasn't by chance. He was sensational.

"Physically he couldn't bring anything to the team. He was small and skinny, but when he had the ball at his feet he had a tremendously competitive spirit."

Then, still only 16 and yet to feature even for the club's reserve side, Messi was given his chance to play for Barcelona's first team.

Fine performance

Frank Rijkaard, Barca's head coach, was looking for squad players to boost numbers for a friendly against Porto in November 2003 and Messi – on Gratacos' recommendation – was one of those chosen by the Dutchman.

Messi only played the last quarter-of-an-hour of the match against the Portuguese side, but proved he was not out of his depth at that level with a fine performance.

Following his brief taste of first-team action, Messi then returned to Barcelona's reserve side to continue improving his skills, while at the same time joining up with the senior squad for training sessions on an increasingly regular basis.

Then, in October 2004, at the age of 17, Rijkaard deemed Messi ready to make his competitive debut for Barcelona in the derby against Espanyol – marking the start of what has become a legendary career.

THE BIG TIME

Messi may have been the young kid on the La Liga block, but he was head and shoulders above most of his opponents in terms of talent.

The question that still had to be answered was whether Messi could make the massive step up to first-team football? He would now be playing against men much older, much bigger and much more experienced than him. Could he fulfil the remarkable promise he had been showing since he was a kid in Argentina? The answer to those questions has been a definite yes.

Such was his potential that Barcelona had no problems making Messi the second youngest player ever to appear for their first team when he took the field in the local derby against Espanyol.

Seven months later Messi earned himself another place in Barcelona history by becoming the club's youngest ever goalscorer. He achieved that against Albacete on May 1, 2005, when he picked up a scooped pass from Brazil star Ronaldinho before coolly lobbing the keeper. The Messi goal

machine was up and running, and the record books were about to take a hammering.

As the months passed, Messi became stronger, more settled among the first-team superstars at Barca, and with it his influence started to grow. In his first season he played a small role as Barcelona became Spanish champions for the first time since 1999. He became more important the following year, 2006, as he helped the "Blaugrana" retain their league title and also reach the final of the Champions League.

Lengthy injury

That was the first time Barcelona had got to the European final since 1994, but although they lifted the trophy with victory over Arsenal, Messi was left out of the matchday squad. That was a huge disappointment for the Argentinian, who had been fit for the final after recovering from a lengthy injury. But, like in all good stories, there were always going to be setbacks and disappointments along the way. Injuries were a major frustration for Messi as his career developed, especially problems with his hamstrings. He was also criticised after punching the ball into the net during Barcelona's derby against Espanyol in 2007 – and getting away with it! That is not something Messi will look back on with pride, unlike two other games around the same time which showed the very best of him.

Still only a teenager, Messi proved there was something very special about him when he scored a stunning hat-trick for Barca

Celebrating becoming Barca's youngest ever goalscorer, against Albacete in 2005.

continued on page 16

Messi celebrates his first hat-trick by kissing the Barcelona shirt – and it was against deadly rivals Real Madrid.

The Club World Cup made it an incredible six competitions out of six for Barcelona in 2009.

continued from page 14

against their arch-rivals Real Madrid in a 3-3 draw. A month later, he then netted what could go down as the greatest goal of his career. It came against Getafe in a Copa del Rey (Spanish Cup) match and saw him run from inside his own half, beating half the opposition defence and also the keeper before putting the ball into the back of the net.

Messi continued to go from strength to strength in the following seasons, but while his star was on the rise, things were not going quite so well for Barcelona as a team. From being champions of Europe and Spain in 2006, they suddenly found themselves without a single trophy for the next two years.

It was a team on the decline, but that was all about to change when Pep Guardiola replaced Frank Rijkaard as head coach in the summer of 2008. Guardiola, the former Barcelona captain who had also come up through the youth ranks, decided changes were needed. One of the biggest changes was allowing Ronaldinho – voted as the best player in the world in 2004 and 2005 – to leave and give his coveted number 10 shirt to Messi, who had previously worn number 19. It was a huge honour and show of faith by Guardiola in the young Argentinian... and Messi did not let him down.

With the likes of Andres Iniesta and Xavi helping to get the very best out of Messi, Barcelona enjoyed the most successful period in their history as they won an astonishing 14 trophies in just four seasons under Guardiola. The highlight was in 2009 when they won all six tournaments they entered – the Primera Division, Champions League, Copa del Rey, Spanish Supercup, European Supercup and Club World Cup.

Swamped with silverware

Messi played crucial roles in all those successes and as Barca found themselves swamped with silverware, he was finally recognised as the best player on the planet when he won the Ballon d'Or award for the first time in 2009. Most worrying for his rivals, Messi insisted in 2010 that there was still more to come from him.

"I don't think I've reached my peak yet. My aim is to keep improving day by day. I want to keep on growing (as a player)," he said.

And grow he did. In the years that followed, his rivalry with Cristiano Ronaldo for the accolade of being named the world's best player gripped the football world – with Messi picking up the Ballon d'Or on four occasions. It didn't take long before people were starting to talk about him as being the best player of all time.

Messi wore the number 19 shirt when he first made it into the Barcelona team, but he inherited the famous number 10 when Brazil star Ronaldinho left the club.

And in 2009 he was to succeed double winner Ronaldinho as world player of the year for the first time – and show off his fashion sense!

YOUTH CLUB

With his career at Barcelona quickly gathering pace, Messi announced himself on the world stage in the 2005 FIFA World Youth Championship.

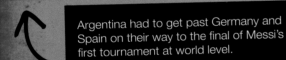

Argentina had to get past Germany and Spain on their way to the final of Messi's first tournament at world level.

Messi had made his Under-20 debut for Argentina in a friendly the year before, but was still to make his full debut for his country's senior team.

He was selected in his nation's squad to compete at the 2005 FIFA World Youth Championship, later called the Under-20 World Cup, that was taking place in Holland – and it was there that Messi made people outside Spain and Argentina really sit up and take notice.

However, the tournament could not have got off to a much worse start, as coach Francisco Ferraro's side lost 1-0 to the United States. Messi started on the bench – alongside teenage striker Sergio Aguero – and was sent on at the start of the second half, but it made no difference.

Argentina's second group game was against Egypt and, with Messi this time starting, he opened the scoring with his first goal of the competition just after half-time. Captain Pablo Zabaleta – later to star for Manchester City with Aguero – then added a second goal late on to secure a 2-0 victory.

Mazy runs

A 1-0 victory over Germany came next, although Messi failed to score and was subbed late in the game. That result meant Argentina finished second in their group and were through to the knockout stages.

Messi, already catching the eye with his fast, mazy runs and close ball control, produced his second goal of the tournament in a 2-1 win over Colombia in the second round. He won the ball himself, played a one-two as he burst into the area, escaped a challenge and fired home.

In the quarter-finals, Argentina met a Spain side boasting the likes of Cesc Fabregas and David Silva, but again they proved too strong and

Messi scores from the spot in the final against Nigeria and celebrates his first honour at international level.

triumphed 3-1. Messi netted the third goal of the tournament with a well-taken finish – just one day after his 18th birthday. Not a bad present!

And so it was Brazil, Argentina's great rivals, who lay in wait in the semi-finals. Messi showed no fear as he opened the scoring early on in a dramatic 2-1 win, picking up the ball 25 yards out, taking a couple of touches inside and firing into the top corner for his fourth goal.

Golden Boot

Messi had inspired his nation to reach the final, where they would meet Nigeria, and he was not about to stop there. Shortly before half-time, he picked up the ball near the halfway line and set off on a trademark run that eventually saw him fouled in the area. He picked himself up and slotted home the resulting penalty.

Nigeria had no answer to Messi and he was upended again in the 75th minute before once more sending the goalkeeper the wrong way from the penalty spot to clinch a 2-1 victory – Argentina were the Under-20 World Cup champions for a fifth time.

It was Messi's first honour at international level, while his six goals earned him the Golden Boot and his performances secured the Golden Ball award that was handed to the star player, an accolade Argentina legend Diego Maradona himself won back in 1979.

EL CHAMPION 1

A glittering array of superstars have contributed to Barcelona's domination over recent years, including the likes of Ronaldinho, Samuel Eto'o, Xavi and Andres Iniesta, but the stand-out performer has undoubtedly been Messi.

Barcelona were without a Primera Division title in five years when Messi made his first-team debut in 2004, but in the subsequent 11 seasons the Catalan giants have gone on to become the most revered club side in world football, collecting the Spanish league title on a staggering seven occasions.

The first of those came in the 2004/05 season, although the young Messi only had a small hand in that success, with one goal from eight appearances, most of them as a substitute.

He made a much bigger contribution the following year, as Barcelona retained their title in emphatic fashion, finishing 12 points clear of their nearest rivals Real Madrid. That season Messi struck six times in 17 league games, and would almost certainly have got many more goals but for an injury that sidelined him for the final few months of the season.

Barcelona were then beaten to the title by Real Madrid for the next two seasons, despite Messi becoming an increasingly dominant force in the game with a series of superb performances.

After going two years without winning any competition, Barcelona decided to replace head coach Frank Rijkaard with Pep Guardiola in the summer of 2008. That marked the start of the greatest period in the club's history – with Messi central to their record-breaking success.

In the next three years, Barcelona would claim trophy after trophy, including three successive Primera Division titles.

In the 2008/09 season, they finished nine points clear of second-placed Real Madrid in a campaign that saw them score an incredible 105 goals. Messi grabbed 23 of them in 31 appearances.

Hottest property

The following season Messi scored 34 goals in 35 matches as Barca retained their title with a 99-point haul, losing just once in 38 games all season. Messi finished as the leading scorer in both the Primera Division and in Europe for the first time in his career, as well as equalling the club-record 34 goals Ronaldo scored for Barcelona in 1996/97.

Messi was now firmly established as the hottest property in the game and he was back among the goals in 2010/11 as Barcelona claimed a hat-trick of league titles.

Messi gets a champagne shower from team-mate Gerard Pique as they celebrate the 2008/09 title.

Messi addresses the fans as Barcelona celebrate the 2009/2010 championship, before showing off the trophy with club president Joan Laporta at a pre-season friendly in August.

The Argentinian found the back of the net 31 times in 33 league games, although he was outscored by Real Madrid superstar Cristiano Ronaldo, who scored 40 goals that season.

All things must come to an end however, and although Messi himself was in record-breaking goalscoring form during the 2011/12 season, Barcelona were unable to win a fourth successive league title. Jose Mourinho's Real Madrid took their crown after becoming the first team in the history of La Liga to reach 100 points in a single campaign.

For Messi, though, this was the start of the most phenomenal 12 months by any player in history. The Argentinian was simply unstoppable, setting record after record as Barcelona – under new coach Tito Vilanova (following the departure of Guardiola in the summer of 2012) – romped to the La Liga title.

At the start of 2012, Messi was awarded FIFA's Ballon d'Or as world player of the year for the third time in a row.

A trademark lob over the goalkeeper was one of an incredible five goals scored against German team Bayer Leverkusen – the first player ever to strike that many in a Champions League game.

SIMPLY THE BEST

The year of 2012 may have been a disappointing one for Barcelona, losing their Champions League and Premiera Division titles, but for Messi it was a personal triumph.

Not content to settle for what had gone before, Messi somehow found an extra gear and started re-writing the record books almost on a monthly basis. It started, as was becoming usual, with Messi being named the world's best player in FIFA's Ballon d'Or awards, winning the crown for the third successive year.

Then, after marking his 200th league appearance for Barcelona with four goals in a 5-1 win over Valencia, Messi scored his first hat-trick for Argentina in an international friendly win over Switzerland.

In March of 2012, Messi was celebrating two more amazing feats. He became the first player to score five times in a Champions League game,

as Barcelona thrashed Bayer Leverkusen 7-1. Then another Primera Division hat-trick, against Granada, saw him become Barcelona's all-time leading goalscorer in official games – at the age of just 24.

His second strike in that game saw him move on to 233 competitive goals for the club, one more than the previous record set by Cesar Rodriguez during the 1940s and 50s. Barca coach Guardiola said: "We are witnessing the best player in every sense. He does everything, and he does it every three days."

Messi was not finished there, though. Not by a long way. He scored all four goals in the 4-0 derby

> ## "My record stood for 40 years and now the best player in the world has broken it, and I'm delighted for him."
>
> – Former West Germany striker Gerd Muller.

Messi celebrates his second goal against Granada in March 2012, which made him Barcelona's all-time record scorer – at the age of just 24.

demolition of Espanyol in May to finish the 2011/12 Primera Division season with a staggering 50 goals.

That was the most in Spanish history and also the most by a player to win the European Golden Shoe as the top scorer in Europe.

The goals continued to fly in as the year progressed, including another Argentina hat-trick, this time against arch-rivals Brazil, as Messi raced his way towards another long-standing record.

An incredible player

That was broken on December 9 when two goals against Real Betis saw Messi beat former West Germany and Bayern Munich striker Gerd Muller's record of 85 goals in a calendar year that he achieved in 1972. Muller said: "My record stood for 40 years – 85 goals in 60 games – and now the best player in the

world has broken it, and I'm delighted for him. He is an incredible player, gigantic."

Messi ended 2012 with 91 goals in all competitions for club and country, including nine hat-tricks, and the end of the year did not stop Messi's one-man attack on the record books either. His amazing exploits in 2012 inevitably saw him named as the best player in the world for the fourth successive time at the start of 2013 after again winning the FIFA Ballon d'Or – something nobody else has ever done.

But Messi's record-breaking antics did not end there. He continued his red-hot form to claim another place in the history books by becoming the first player ever to score in consecutive Primera Division matches against every other team in the division after netting for the 19th successive league game in a 2-2 draw with Celta Vigo.

EL CHAMPION 2

Between the 2012/13 and 2018/19 seasons, Lionel Messi was in incredible form as Barcelona dominated Spanish football and wrapped up another five La Liga titles.

Helped in no small part by Messi's red-hot form in front of goal, Barcelona romped to their 22nd La Liga title in 2012/13, losing only twice en route to finishing a massive 15 points clear of archrivals Real Madrid. Messi led the way in the league in both the goalscoring charts (with 46 goals – 12 more than Cristiano Ronaldo) and with assists (12). Barcelona reached the semi-finals in both the Champions League and the Copa del Rey, losing to Bayern Munich in the former and to Real Madrid in the latter.

Barcelona and Messi, under new coach Gerardo Martino, got their 2013/14 campaign off to a blistering start. On August 18, 2013, the opening game of the season, Messi chipped in with two goals and an assist in a 7-0 demolition of Levante. Two weeks later, Barcelona secured their first silverware of the season, beating Atletico Madrid on away goals to win the Supercopa de Espagna.

Treble joy

Having committed his long-term future to the club at the end of the previous season, Messi started the 2014/15 campaign as he had the previous one, by scoring two goals in Barcelona's opening game – this time a 3-0 victory over Elche. On September 27, 2014, he scored his 400th professional goal (still only 27 years of age); two weeks later, he netted twice in a 3-0 home victory over SD Eibar – it was his 250th goal in La Liga, taking him to within one goal of Telmo Zarra's all-time La Liga record haul of 251 goals. He surpassed Zarra's record when he scored a hat-trick in Barca's 5–1 rout of Sevilla on November 22.

Whatever disappointment Messi must have felt after missing out on top honours in the 2014 FIFA Ballon d'Or, he did not show; instead, his magical form propelled Barcelona to a season to remember. On May 17, he scored the only goal of the game against Atletico Madrid to secure the league title. Two weeks later, he scored twice in Barcelona's 3-1 victory over Athletic Club at the Nou Camp to win the domestic double for the second time in his career. But the best was still to come.

Messi had played a starring role in Barcelona's imperious march to the Champions League final, notably with two goals and an assist in Barca's 3-0 semi-final first-leg victory over Bayern Munich. In the final, against Juventus at the Olympiastadion in Berlin, he had a hand in all three of Barca's goals in a 3-1 victory.

Messi's team-mates congratulate the Argentinian maestro as he became La Liga's all-time leading goalscorer.

The Argentinian top scored in La Liga in 2018/19 as Barça won their 26th league title.

Messi had a hand in all three of Barcelona's goals as they won the 2015 Champions League final.

It was the same story in 2015/16 as Messi continued to rip apart defences in Spain and although Barcelona surrendered their Champions League title, they were unstoppable in La Liga and the Copa del Rey. Messi scored 26 goals in the league as Luis Enrique's side were crowned champions for the 24th time, while he was on target five times in five appearances to take Barca to the final of the Copa del Rey, beating Sevilla 2-0 in extra time.

The goals kept coming in both 2017/18 and 2018/19 as Messi netted an incredible 70 goals in La Liga to give Barcelona two more tittles and the Argentinian his 10th league winner's medal. The star was again top scorer in Spain in both remarkable seasons while his haul took him past the fabled 400 league goals for the Catalans. He was also on target in the 2018 Copa del Rey final against Sevilla as Barça romped to a 5-0 victory to secure an eighth Spanish league and cup double.

GREAT GOALS 1

Messi's career has been highlighted by loads of brilliant goals – some individual and some thanks to great teamwork. Here's a selection of the best:

BARCELONA 5 GETAFE 2
Spanish Copa del Rey, April 18, 2007

Messi has scored many memorable goals for club and country, but his amazing strike against Getafe in the Spanish Cup will take some beating.

Diego Maradona's famous second goal for Argentina in the 1986 World Cup quarter-final win over England is considered by many to be the best goal of all time, and Messi produced an almost identical effort for Barcelona 21 years later.

Picking up the ball five metres inside his own half the twinkle-toed magician skipped past two opposing defenders as he raced over the halfway line, and accelerated towards the edge of the Getafe box, where he evaded two more desperate attempts to stop him. There was still work to do, but Messi was not to be denied his wonder goal, cleverly rounding the goalkeeper before neatly dinking a right-footed shot over a sliding defender on the line.

Messi volleys into an empty net to complete his brilliant Champions League goal against Arsenal.

Messi was still in his own half when he started to twist and turn past Getafe defenders...

BARCELONA 3 ARSENAL 1
Champions League, March 8, 2011

Many of Messi's best goals show just how good he is in all areas of the game. He can score many types of goal. Sometimes it is a mazy run, or a quick burst of pace or a powerful shot.

Messi gets much of the praise, but it is easy to forget that he is actually a member of one of the best sides ever at Barcelona. His team-mates have also played big parts in many of Messi's goals, and one example of that was against Arsenal in a Champions League match at the Nou Camp.

The match was deep into injury time at the end of the first half when Andres Iniesta made the most of a mistake by Cesc Fabregas. Iniesta pinched the ball off the Arsenal midfielder and then produced a wonderful little pass to put Messi through inside the area. That was brilliant by Iniesta, but even better was to come from Messi. The Barcelona number 10 neatly controlled the ball before showing outrageous skill and confidence to loft the ball over Gunners keeper Manuel Almunia and volley into an empty net.

REAL MADRID 0 BARCELONA 2

Champions League, April 27, 2011

Messi has enjoyed some memorable matches against Barca's arch-rivals Real Madrid down the years, and this was another one as he scored both goals in a famous Champions League victory at the Bernabeu.

His second, in the 87th minute, was a wonderful individual goal. He evaded the attentions of four Madrid defenders as he raced into the penalty area before sliding a low right-footed shot past Iker Casillas.

Messi slides his shot past Real Madrid defender Sergio Ramos and into the back of the net.

ATLETICO MADRID 1 BARCELONA 2

Primera Division, February 26, 2012

Messi is not only fantastic at dribbling and beating defenders, he is also pretty special from free-kicks.

One of his most memorable was against Atletico Madrid, when Messi showed both tremendous quick-thinking but also fantastic skill to earn Barcelona an 81st-minute winner at the Vicente Calderon.

Standing over a free-kick on the left corner of the penalty area, Messi spotted Atletico goalkeeper Thibaut Courtois still lining up his wall. The Argentinian took advantage to fire in a curling shot that found the top far right corner of the net with Courtois helpless.

Messi celebrates his cheeky free-kick against Atletico Madrid.

Nov 16 2003
Makes first-team debut in a friendly at Porto, aged 16.

Oct 16, 2004
Appears in first official match for Barcelona in the 1-0 derby win over Espanyol. At the age of 17 years, three months and 22 days, Messi becomes the second-youngest player to play a league game for Barcelona's first team.

May 1 2005
Becomes youngest player to score for Barcelona in La Liga with his goal against Albacete.

March 10, 2007
Scores first senior hat-trick for club at age 19 and does it in style against Barcelona's arch-rivals Real Madrid at the Nou Camp. All of Messi's goals were equalisers with the final one coming in the last minute and earning Barcelona, who were down to 10 men, a 3-3 draw.

March 20, 2012
Becomes Barcelona's all-time leading goalscorer after scoring twice against Granada in La Liga. His second goal of the match saw him move on to 233 official goals, one more than the previous record set by Cesar Rodriguez during the 1940s and 50s.

May 27, 2009
Messi's header against Manchester United helped Barcelona win the Champions League title and in the process secure their first-ever treble, having already won the league and cup titles that season.

Nov 22, 2014
Scores hat-trick in Barcelona's 5–1 victory over Sevilla to become the La Liga's all-time leading goalscorer (with 253 goals).

June 6, 2015
Plays a part in all three goals as Barcelona beat Juventus 3–1 in the Champions League final - victory sees Barca become the only team in history to win the treble twice.

April 17, 2016
Messi scores his 500th career goal for club and country against Valencia in La Liga.

Oct 18, 2017
The Argentinean is on target in the UEFA Champions League group stage game against Olympiakos. It is his 100th career goal in UEFA club competitions.

Jan 7, 2018
He makes his 400th appearance in La Liga against Levante and marks the occasion with his 365th league goal for Barcelona, equalling Gerd Müller's record for most league goals in one of Europe's top five divisions.

May 1, 2019
Messi nets at the Nou Camp against Liverpool in the UEFA Champions League semi-final with a 35-yard free-kick – the 600th goal of his Barcelona career.

OLYMPIC GOLD

Messi's greatest international achievement to date came in 2008 when he helped lead Argentina to the gold medal at the Beijing Olympic Games.

Messi's chance to be involved in Beijing was in doubt right up until his nation's opening game of the tournament. The day before, Barcelona won a court battle against FIFA, who insisted that clubs must release players under the age of 23 for the Games.

That meant Barcelona could stop Messi playing, but he was picked to start for Argentina against the Ivory Coast and swept home the opening goal just before half-time before setting up Lautaro Acosta's late winner in a 2-1 triumph. It was only after the match that it was revealed Messi had asked to stay at the Olympics in a chat with Barcelona's new coach Pep Guardiola, who allowed the 21-year-old to stay in China and compete for his country.

Messi failed to find the net in the subsequent 1-0 win over Australia and, with Argentina safely through to the quarter-finals, he was left on the bench for a 2-0 victory over Serbia.

But, as at the Under-20 World Cup three years earlier, he had already shown the kind of skills that were capturing the imagination of the football world amid a talented Argentina side boasting the likes of Pablo Zabaleta, Juan Riquelme, Javier Mascherano, Sergio Aguero and Angel Di Maria.

Holland were the opposition in the quarter-finals and Messi was again on the scoresheet, charging down a loose ball before bursting through on the edge of the penalty area and going round the keeper to score.

Great through-ball

The match went to extra time though, before Messi was involved in the winner as he set up Di Maria with a great through-ball to clinch a tough 2-1 victory.

As in 2005, Brazil and Nigeria stood in the way of success, but their great South American rivals – led by recently-departed Barca team-mate Ronaldinho – proved little test in the semi-finals as Argentina easily triumphed 3-0.

Messi, in arguably the biggest game of his international career, did not disappoint in the Olympic final against Nigeria, capping a fine individual display with the pass for Di Maria's match-winning second-half chip.

Argentina had successfully defended their Olympic crown – and gold medallist Messi was the star of the show.

Messi consoles former Barcelona team-mate Ronaldinho, who was captain of Brazil, after the semi-final.

It's a golden moment as Messi (far left) dances on the top step of the podium in the Olympic medal ceremony and then kisses his precious gold medal.

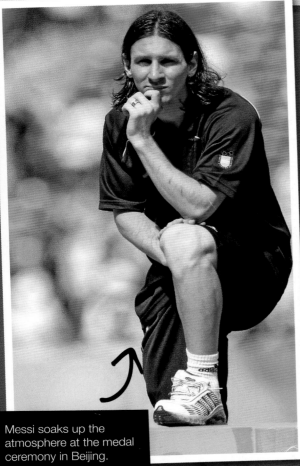

Messi soaks up the atmosphere at the medal ceremony in Beijing.

OFF DUTY

Messi is all-action on the pitch and rarely misses a match, but the superstar knows how to relax when he does get some time off from football.

Messi has three children, Thiago (born 2012), Mateo (born 2015) and Ciro (born 2018).

Messi married his childhood sweetheart Antonela in his hometown of Rosario in the summer of 2017.

Messi and his fans at the launch of the latest version of the Messi boots brand made by adidas.

Lionel Messi attracts a gaggle of well-wishers, even though he's just out and about doing a spot of shopping.

Messi, with his children and Luis Suárez, watch Barça from the stands.

Messi relaxes with family and friends on a luxury yacht far away from the constant media attention that follows a superstar footballer.

EUROSTAR

Barcelona had only won one European Cup title in their history – against Sampdoria at Wembley back in 1992 – before Messi's arrival at the Nou Camp, but that statistic was soon about to change.

The first of the four Champions League winner's medals Messi has won so far came in 2006. Despite still being a teenager, he was a regular in Barcelona's team for the early part of the tournament and scored against Greek side Panathinaikos in the group stages.However, he suffered a thigh injury during the quarter-final against Chelsea and was deemed unfit to play in the final, in which Barcelona beat another English side, Arsenal, 2-1 in Paris.

Messi was bitterly disappointed not to have been involved in that game, but he got another chance in 2009 after helping Barcelona reach the final again, and he was determined not to waste the opportunity.

Messi scored nine goals in the competition that season, but his most important by far was his header in the final that sealed a 2-0 victory over Manchester United in Rome.

Barcelona were knocked out at the semi-final stage the following year, losing to eventual winners Inter Milan, but the Nou Camp club did not have to wait much longer to get their hands on the trophy again as Messi earned his third winner's medal in 2011 – and Manchester United were again the victims.

Messi netted in every round, including both goals as Barcelona beat rivals Real Madrid 2-0 away from home in the semi-finals, and he was again on the scoresheet in the final as his side triumphed 3-1 over United at Wembley.

Back on top

Messi was unable to inspire another Champions League final appearance in either 2012, 2013 or 2014 as Barcelona were dumped out first by Chelsea and then by Bayern Munich (in the semi-finals) and then by Atletico Madrid (in the quarter-finals).

But it was an altogether different story in 2015. On 25 November, he scored a hat-trick against APOEL to become the competition's all-time leading goalscorer. Typically, Messi shone for Barcelona when it really mattered. Barcelona marched through the competition and faced Bayern Munich in the semi-finals. The Germans held firm for 77 minutes in the first leg at the Camp Nou, before Messi scored twice and provided an assist in a 3-0 victory that rendered the contest effectively over. He played a part in all three of Barcelona's goals in the final, too, as the Catalans eased to a 3-1 victory over Juventus in Berlin. It was the Argentinian's fourth Champions League winner's medal – and it seems as though there will be plenty more of them to come.

Barcelona fans let Messi go to their heads as they arrive at Wembley Stadium for the 2011 Champions League final against Manchester United.

Manchester United goalkeeper Edwin van der Sar looks horrified as little Messi gets up to head the second goal in the 2009 final.

Back home in Barcelona, Messi gets in the party mood with his victorious Barca team-mates.

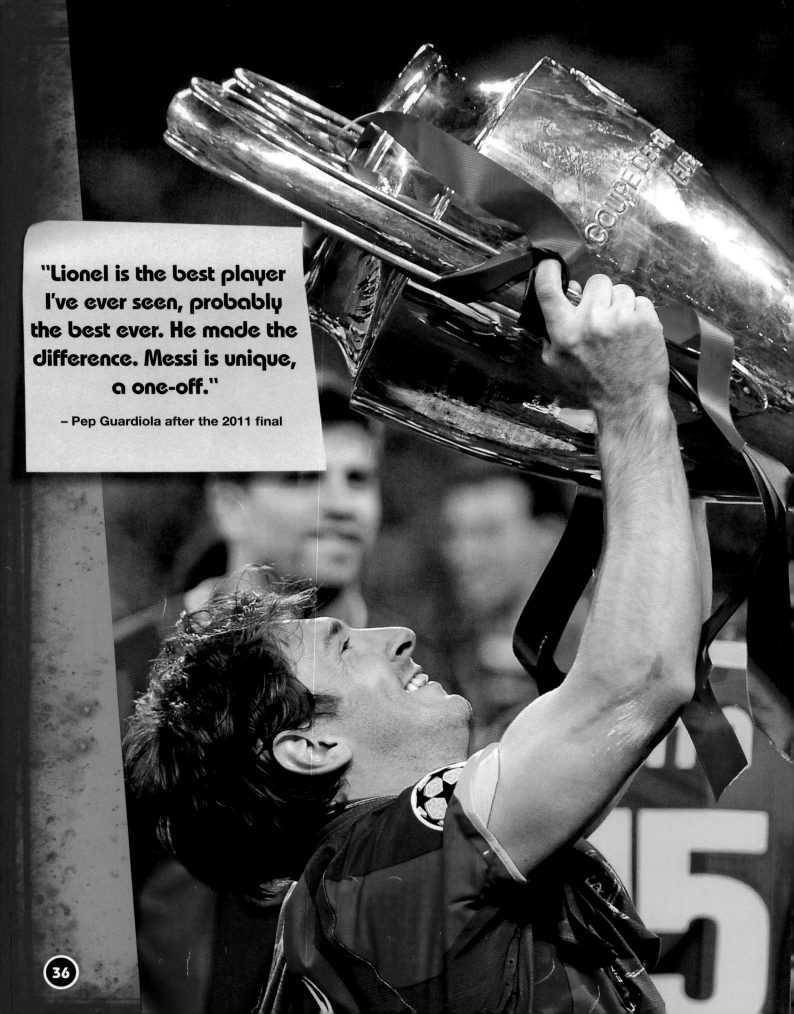

"Lionel is the best player I've ever seen, probably the best ever. He made the difference. Messi is unique, a one-off."

– Pep Guardiola after the 2011 final

CHAMPION AGAIN

Messi was on target again when Barcelona and Manchester United came face to face once more in the 2011 Champions League final, this time at Wembley. He got one of the goals in Barca's 3-1 victory – and celebrated in typical fashion.

(From left to right): The Barcelona forward line of Suarez, Messi and Neymar was too hot to handle for most of the Catalan's Champions League opponents in 2014–15.

EXPERT VIEW

Messi has enthralled and amazed football fans all over the world with his silky skills and awesome ability, but he has also made a huge impression on his fellow professionals. Here's what they say about him:

Tito Vilanova
Former Barcelona coach

"We do not know his limits. You should see how he trains every day – that urge he has to keep getting better. I think we will never see another player like this. He is the best in the world by far."

Samuel Eto'o
Cameroon striker and Barcelona team-mate between 2004 and 2009

"Messi is a God – as a person and even more so as a player. I hope that he wins the World Cup with Argentina. To the Gods of the world, all I ask is that you give him that chance."

Thierry Henry
World Cup winner and Barcelona team-mate between 2007 and 2010

"Every player on the planet is in Messi's shadow. If you want to step out of Messi's shadow, try another sport."

David Villa
Former Barcelona team-mate and Spain's all-time leading international goalscorer

"He is doing incredible things. Each day he surprises everyone with a new record, he continually outdoes himself. Nobody can compare with him."

Messi with strike partners Thierry Henry (above) and David Villa. (below).

Ossie Ardiles
Former Spurs and Argentina midfield star

"For some time I thought Diego Maradona could never be surpassed, and nor could Pele, but no longer. I would now say that Lionel Messi will go down in history as the number one player of all time, the best that there ever was."

Ronaldo
Former Barcelona and Brazil striker, and world player of the year in 1996, 1997 and 2002

"He has so much creativity, he enchants us. And despite the fact that he's Argentinian, the great rivals of Brazil, he's a player who I admire a great deal. He is the best in the world, so far ahead of the rest. I wish I was 10 years younger so I could play with Messi."

Arsène Wenger
Former Arsenal manager, against whose team Messi scored all four goals in a 4-1 Champions League victory in 2010

"Messi is like a PlayStation player. He can punish any mistake, make a difference at any moment."

Lionel Messi and Andres Iniesta celebrate with the trophy following Barcelona's 3-0 defeat of River Plate in the FIFA Club World Cup final in December 2015.

Iker Casillas

FIFA World Cup winner, UEFA European Championship winner and former Real Madrid and Spain goalkeeper

"The best striker I have ever faced? Lionel Messi. It has always been Lionel Messi."

Carles Puyol

Barcelona team-mate 2004–14, FIFA World Cup 2010 and UEFA EURO 2008 winner with Spain

"This Barca will be remembered as Messi's Barca. He's well above anything else I've ever seen. He's an alien."

Andres Iniesta

2010 World Cup winner, Barcelona's former captain and team-mate 2004–18

"His skill, the essence of him as a player, has always been there for all to see. Leo Messi does things that nobody else does."

GREAT GOALS 2

Domestic competition, Champions League or international football – it doesn't matter to Messi, who can score fantastic goals anywhere.

ARGENTINA 4 BRAZIL 3

International friendly, June 9, 2012

Does it get much better than this? Playing against your biggest rivals, five minutes to go, the game locked at 3-3 and if you score one more goal you complete your hat-trick and win the game.

Even a tap-in would have been a fairytale end to the game, but the wizard Messi conjured up something just a little more special.

Messi's first two goals in the game weren't bad, but his third, the match-winner, was simply brilliant. There appeared little danger as he was given the ball out wide near the halfway line, but he immediately skipped past a Brazil defender before racing full speed towards the penalty area.

Then, 25 yards out from goal, he unleashed an unstoppable left-footed thunderbolt that flew into the far top corner of the net with Brazil goalkeeper Rafael Barbosa rooted to the spot.

BARCELONA 4 REAL BETIS 2

Primera Division, May 5, 2013

Another perfect example of how Messi can score unforgettable team goals as well as individual goals came in the league match against Real Betis.

Barcelona were leading 3-2 when three of their forward players combined to devastating effect to add a fourth goal and seal the win.

Alexis Sanchez started the move with a pass into Messi near the edge of the penalty box. Messi then played the ball on to Andres Iniesta, whose fantastic back-heel returned the ball to Alexis who had run into the area.

Alexis could have shot himself, but he decided to play an inch-perfect pass across goal to Messi, who had got in behind the Betis defence to side-foot home at the far post.

Three players, eight seconds, nine touches, goal. Simply unstoppable.

Messi beats Brazil defender Juan to score his brilliant third goal and clinch a 4-3 win.

Alexis Sanchez and Andres Iniesta rush to celebrate with Messi after they all played key roles in a great team goal against Real Betis.

BARCELONA 4 AC MILAN 0
Champions League, March 12, 2013

Barcelona looked to be on their way out of the Champions League at the hands of AC Milan after losing the first leg 2-0 in Italy, but Messi had other ideas. He started the fightback with a brilliant goal in the fifth minute of the second leg.

Six different players were involved as Barca moved the ball and looked to drag their opponents out of position. Then, in the blink of an eye, the ball was in the back of the net as Messi played a quick one-two with Xavi on the edge of the box before unleashing a superb curling shot into the top corner of the net. Messi scored again before half-time and Barcelona went on to win 4-0.

Messi celebrates with team-mates Dani Alves, Jordi Alba, David Villa and Andres Iniesta after scoring against AC Milan.

GREAT MATES

Messi is always the centre of attention, but football is a team game, and he is part of possibly the greatest side ever to play the game.

While Messi has established himself as the world's top player, he admits he would not have achieved the success he has without the help of his team-mates.

He said: "I'm lucky that I get to play here at Barca and for Argentina, where I get to play with fantastic players. They have given me everything: the individual awards, the titles, the goals, everything. Without the help of my team-mates, I would be nothing."

A lot of his colleagues at Barcelona (both past and present) have played together for many years, having graduated from the club's famous La Masia academy. Messi explained: "The Barca philosophy isn't about just one coach or another, it's based on an idea, a line that is laid down and all coaches follow. That has always been the way in which the club has worked with the academy."

Such has been the success of Barcelona's youth policy that eight of the players involved in their 2009 Champions League final win over Manchester United had all been at the club as youngsters.

Hugely successful

Messi said: "We've been playing together for a long time and we virtually know where the ball's going two or three passes in advance."

The same style of football has also been hugely successful for the Spanish national team, which is little surprise when lots of Barcelona players also play for their country.

Messi has been lucky to play with some of the game's greatest players during his record-breaking Nou Camp career. Between 2014 and 2017, he formed a deadly attacking force with fellow South Americans, the Brazilian Neymar and Luis Suárez from Uruguay. In just three seasons together, the trio scored an incredible 364 goals between them.

More recently he has teamed up with French World Cup winner Ousmane Dembélé, star Croatian midfielder Ivan Rakitić, Chilean hero Arturo Vidal and, in 2018/19, another notable Brazilian in Philippe Coutinho as Barcelona have continued to dominate Spanish football.

Messi has formed a prolific partnership with Luis Suarez since the deadly duo teamed up at the Nou Camp in 2014.

Messi and defender Gerard Pique have grown up together from the La Masia academy.

"I'm lucky that I get to play here at Barça and for Argentina, where I get to play with fantastic players. They have given me everything."

THAT'S A FACT 2

August 17, 2005
Messi's debut for the senior Argentina team lasted less than 60 seconds! The 18-year-old wonderkid had just come on when his shirt was being pulled by Vilmos Vanczak. Messi threw his arm back and the defender went down holding his face. Messi was shown a red card and was soon in tears back in the dressing room.

A heartbroken Messi walks off after getting a red card within a minute of coming on for his international debut.

June 16, 2006
Messi stepped off the bench in the group game against Serbia and Montenegro to become the youngest ever Argentina player to appear at the World Cup, aged 18 years and 357 days. He then scored the final goal in a 6-0 victory to ensure he was, at the time, the sixth youngest player to ever score in the tournament.

August 2011
Messi is named the captain of Argentina at the age of 24 by new manager Alejandro Sabella.

June–July 2014
Captains Argentina at the 2014 World Cup in Brazil. He is voted Man of the Match in all three group games as Argentina progress to the final for the first time since 1990, but suffers heartbreak as Mario Götze's 113th-minute strike wins the Cup for Germany.

June 20, 2015
When he wins his 100th cap for Argentina, against Jamaica in the Copa America, Messi becomes only the fifth Argentina player to achieve this amazing milestone.

June 22, 2016
Messi's effort in the 4-0 demolition of hosts United States in the Copa America Centenario takes him to 55 international goals, breaking the Argentina record previously held by Gabriel Batistuta.

Messi became Argentina's all-time top scorer 11 years after making his international debut.

October 10, 2017
Messi scores a brilliant hat-trick against Ecuador to seal a 3-1 victory and book Argentina's place at the 2018 World Cup in Russia. His treble makes him the joint all-time scorer in South American World Cup qualifiers with 21.

June 26, 2018
The star nets in the World Cup group stage fixture against Nigeria in Saint Petersburg. His goal makes Messi only the third Argentinean after Diego Maradona and Gabriel Batistuta to score at three different World Cups.

June 30, 2018
Messi sets up two goals at the FIFA World Cup in the round of 16 tie with France – the fourth consecutive tournament at which he'd provided an assist. But there was no happy ending as France won 4-3.

Messi's strike against Nigeria in Russia in 2018 took his World Cup finals goals tally to six.

NATIONAL HERO

Messi's career in international football with Argentina so far has been a story full of ups and downs – but maybe one day it will have a happy ending.

Compared to the success he has enjoyed with Barcelona, Messi has not managed to do the same with his country – but it could have been very different if he had not stayed loyal to Argentina.

Following his move to Barca and with his potential very clear, Messi was offered the chance to play for Spain, but turned it down in order to wait for his chance with Argentina. He said: "I would have never chosen to play for Spain because I am Argentine."

His senior call-up, aged 18, for a game against Hungary in August 2005 was a moment he had been dreaming of for so long, but it soon turned into a nightmare as the wonderkid was brought off the bench in the 63rd minute and shown a red card less than 60 seconds later – a sending-off that left Messi in tears back in the dressing room.

He made what he described as a "re-debut" a month later before being handed his first senior start against Peru, and then netting his first goal for his country in a friendly against Croatia in March 2006. Legend Diego Maradona labelled Messi as his true successor, saying: "I have seen the player who will inherit my place in Argentine football and his name is Messi."

Although Messi enjoyed glory in the 2008 Olympic Games in Beijing, winning a gold medal with Argentina, the 2006 and 2010 FIFA World Cup and 2007 and 2011 Copa Américas were all hugely disappointing. The quarter-final exit in 2011 was especially galling as Argentina had been the Copa América hosts.

So close

Messi got both his and Argentina's 2014 World Cup finals off to a flying start, netting the second goal in his side's 2-1 opening-game victory over Bosnia and Herzegovina. Argentina went on to reach the final for the first time since 1990, but lost 1-0 to Germany, Mario Götze scoring in extra time to bring both Argentina and Messi's dream to a crushing end. The big prize had eluded him once again.

In June 2016 Argentina were beaten in the Copa America final by Chile and after the final a heartbroken Messi announced he was retiring from international football at the age of 29.

The country was in total shock but after nationwide appeals for him to change his mind, Messi returned to the team in September 2016 and he marked his first game back with the winning goal in a World Cup qualifier against Uruguay.

Despite his return, Argentina's place in the World Cup was hanging by a thread going into their last qualifier, away against Ecuador in October 2017, but a brilliant Messi hat-trick saved the day and a fourth finals beckoned for the Barça star. Argentina's performances in Russia in the summer of 2018 saw the team reach the knockout stages thanks to a Messi goal in a 2-1 win over Nigeria in the final Group D game in Saint Petersburg. They faced France in the round of 16 and although the striker had two assists, he couldn't stop his side slipping to a 4-3 defeat. It was little consolation to both Messi and Argentina that France would go on to win the World Cup a couple of weeks later.

In 2019, Argentina lost to Copa América hosts Brazil in the semi-final. It got worse in the third-place play-off against Chile as Messi was sent off in a 2-1 victory.

Messi scored his first senior international goal, against Croatia in 2006.

"I would have never chosen to play for Spain because I am Argentine."

Messi is now Argentina's record goal scorer and he is on course to be the most capped player in the country's history.

THE WORLD STAGE

Many people believe Messi cannot truly be regarded as one of the all-time best players in football until he has helped his country win the World Cup.

Messi was first selected for World Cup duty in the Argentina squad that travelled to Germany in 2006. After remaining unused for the opening group game, he stepped off the bench in the 75th minute against Serbia and Montenegro. That made him the youngest Argentinian ever to appear at the World Cup, aged 18 years and 357 days.

Messi had already set up one goal when he bagged the last in a 6-0 rout to ensure he again wrote his name in the history books as the sixth youngest player ever to score at the tournament.

Yet disappointment was to follow for both Messi and Argentina in the quarter-finals as they crashed out of the competition to hosts Germany on penalties.

Further misery was to come four years later. After being handed the famous number 10 shirt by the legendary Diego Maradona in what was the first 2010 World Cup qualifier since his sensational appointment as coach, Messi bagged the opener in a comfortable 4-0 win over Venezuela.

But Argentina had a poor qualification campaign and, with Messi scoring only four times, they only scraped through to the tournament in South Africa. Matters did not improve much once there as, despite breezing through to the quarter-finals, Argentina were embarrassed 4-0 by Germany once again.

Messi celebrates after scoring Argentina's final goal in the 6-0 win over Serbia and Montenegro in his first World Cup appearance.

So close to glory

Messi and Argentina would both have had high hopes as they travelled to Brazil for the 2014 World Cup. And when the South Americans eased to the top of their group, with Messi picking up the Man of the Match award in every one of three games, expectation started to grow to fever pitch.

Argentina beat Switzerland in the round of 16 (1-0), Belgium in the quarter-finals (1-0), and Holland (5-4 on penalties) in the semi-finals. But the dream came to an end in the final against Germany – a match billed as the world's best player against the world's best team. Germany won the match 1–0, and yet again Messi was left to ponder what might have been.

Messi's scored his first World Cup finals goal against Serbia and Montenegro in Germany in 2006 finals.

Messi scored against Venezuela in qualifying for the 2010 World Cup after being given the famous number 10 shirt for the first time by new coach Diego Maradona, but Argentina's trip to the finals in South Africa brought more misery.

They got through to the quarter-finals again, but once more Germany stood in their way and this time they powered to a 4-0 win to leave Messi and Argentina distraught.

Messi celebrates scoring against Venezuela in qualifying – his first game in the number 10 shirt for Argentina.

Argentina's 2010 FIFA World Cup 4-0 quarter-final defeat against Germany left Messi bitterly disappointed – and in need of a hug from coach Diego Maradona.

Messi found his goalscoring touch at the 2014 World Cup, but Argentina's World Cup dreams lay in tatters after they lost in the final to Germany.

51

COACH PARTY

Messi has played under several coaches and managers during his club and international career and has not failed to impress any of them.

Pep Guardiola

Led Barcelona to an amazing period of success with 14 trophies in just four seasons and played a key role in helping Messi develop into the best player in the world.

"Like Michael Jordan in basketball, Messi is dominating his sport. Very few people in history have managed to dominate their sport the way Jordan and Messi have.

"I feel sorry for those who want to compete for Messi's throne – it's impossible, this kid is unique. He doesn't just score lots of goals, but he scores lots of great goals, each one being better than the last.

"The throne belongs to him, and no one else but him will decide when he vacates it. He's the best there is. There's no one else. I can count myself lucky to have been his coach."

Former Holland international star Frank Rijkaard was the Barcelona coach who gave Messi his first-team chance.

Frank Rijkaard

Gave Messi his Barcelona debut during his time in charge at the Nou Camp between 2003 and 2008.

"He's an incredible person. Messi is not simply a uniquely talented footballer. He's also strong mentally, very bright and exceptionally dedicated to his job.

"Personally speaking I enjoy watching him play and I'm deeply proud of him and what he has achieved. Quite simply, he's the best."

Messi and Barça boss Ernesto Valverde won back-to-back league titles in their first two seasons working together.

Ernesto Valverde
Appointed Barcelona manager in May 2017.
"Messi does extraordinary things and makes them routine. There are no words to describe Leo Messi. Despite the opposition being on the receiving end, we are all enjoying this era of his, which is unequalled."

"I think it would be a sin not to give Messi to the people, to the team"

– Diego Maradona, Argentina coach 2008–2010

Lionel Scaloni
Appointed Argentina coach in November 2018.
"Messi is Messi. He's the best, above everyone else. The players love Messi so much. He is the best player in the history of football. We are used to him scoring three goals each game or dribbling past five opponents."

GLOBAL SUPERSTAR

Messi is now undeniably the best player in the modern game, and it has made him recognisable all over the world.

His obvious qualities on the pitch as well as his humble and gracious attitude have made Lionel Messi a role model for millions of fans.

The Argentinian has twice been named in *Time* magazine's annual list of the 100 most influential people on the planet. His worldwide fame has seen the star land sponsorship deals with Adidas, Pepsi and computer game company Konami, while he is also a global ambassador for luxury clothes brand Dolce & Gabbana, high-end watch maker Audemars Piguet and Turkish Airlines.

In April 2011, Messi launched a Facebook page that by 2015 had attracted nearly 80 million likes. He also has a Twitter page and an Instagram account and according to a 2016 survey, Messi's social media audience was more than 122 million across all three platforms.

Famous waxwork museum Madame Tussauds has already made a lifesize figure of the Barcelona forward which has been on display to visitors since September 2012. Two years later a documentary, entitled *Messi*, about his incredible journey from Argentina to Spain and his Nou Camp career premiered at the Venice Film Festival.

Goodwill ambassador

Nicknamed "the flea" due to his size, speed and balance, Messi has also been the subject of more wacky adulation including the pure gold replica of

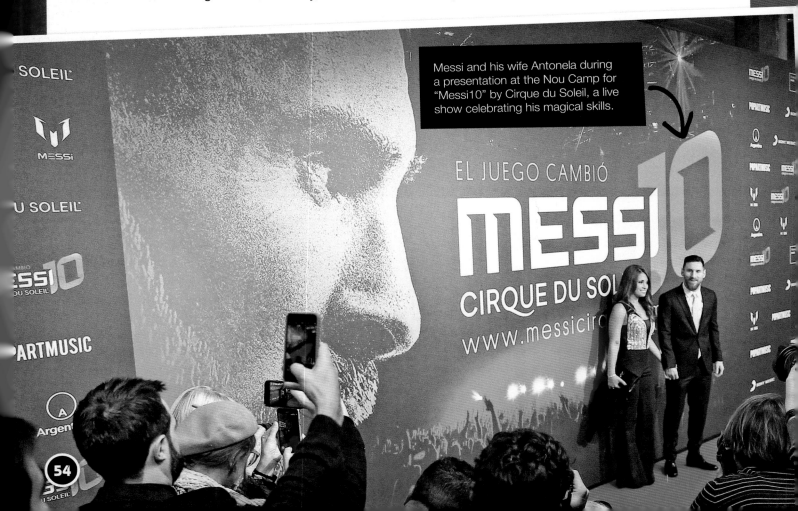

Messi and his wife Antonela during a presentation at the Nou Camp for "Messi10" by Cirque du Soleil, a live show celebrating his magical skills.

Messi also spends much of his free time with charity work and in 2010 he was named as a goodwill ambassador for the United Nations Children's Fund.

his magical left foot on sale in Japan.

Charity work forms a large part of Messi's life, especially helping out kids in need. It includes the Leo Messi Foundation he set up in 2007 to help vulnerable children and his role as a goodwill ambassador for Unicef.

Despite the fact that he is not as well known in the United States, where American Football, baseball, basketball and ice hockey are more popular, Messi still made the headlines in 2011 when President Barack Obama mentioned him in a speech. Then, in 2016, he sent signed shirts to the President's daughters Malia and Sasha after they revealed they were big fans.

GREAT GOALS 3

And the great goals kept on coming from Messi – at the World Cup, in La Liga and in the Champions League. No stage, it seems, is too grand for the Argentinian maestro.

BARCELONA 5 SEVILLA 1
Premiera Division, November 22, 2014

This was not so much the goal itself, but the significance of it. Throughout the early part of the 2014/15 season, Messi had been hunting down Telmo Zarra's all-time goalscoring record in La Liga – 251 goals in a 15-year career for Athletic Bilboa between 1940 and 1955. And as the Argentinian drew closer, the clamour became louder. By the time Barcelona faced Sevilla in La Liga at the Nou Camp on November 22, Messi was just one goal behind. He opened the scoring with a trademark free-kick in the first half to equal the record, and then, in the 71st minute, with Barcelona leading 3-1, he tapped in from short range following a Barca breakaway to set a new mark. His team-mates responded by gathering around Messi, picking him up and hurling him into the air.

SPORTING GIJON 1 BARCELONA 3
La Liga, February 17, 2016

Messi has always done things in style throughout his record-breaking career and it was no different when he became the first ever player to score 300 goals in La Liga. His historic strike came in the 24th minute of the match against Sporting Gijon. He collected the ball 40 yards from goal and beat two defenders with a drop of the shoulder and a trademark burst of pace. Messi was still outside the area but a glorious left-footed drive, which rocketed into the bottom corner, was a typically brilliant effort to take him to the landmark of 300 La Liga goals.

Messi's second goal against Sevilla saw him break Telmo Zarra's all-time La Liga goalscoring record.

Messi's goal against Gijon underlined his status as La Liga's deadliest marksman of all time.

TOTTENHAM HOTSPUR 2
BARCELONA 4

Champions League, October 3, 2018

It was a six-goal thriller at Wembley – Tottenham's temporary home – but Messi was the undisputed star of the show as the superstar tore the Spurs defence to shreds. The Argentinian scored twice and the best of his brilliant brace was his second. Messi started the move 30 metres out with a deft pass and as the Spurs defence were pulled out wide, he ghosted unmarked into the penalty area. A clever dummy by Luis Suárez created the space and Messi delivered the knockout blow with a beautiful side-footed finish past Hugo Lloris into the bottom corner.

Messi was simply unstoppable when Barça thumped Spurs in a 2018/19 UEFA Champions League group game at Wembley.

ADRIANO
21

March 7 2012
Becomes the first player to score five goals in a Champions League game as Barcelona thrash Bayer Leverkusen 7-1.

May 12, 2012
Finishes the season with an incredible 50 goals in the league – a Primera Division record and also beating the previous-best mark to win the European Golden Shoe, which was the 47 goals scored by Romanian Dudu Georgescu for Dinamo Bucharest in 1976/77.

Dec 9, 2012
Breaks the record for the most goals in a calendar year with his double against Real Betis taking him to 86 in all competitions for Barcelona and Argentina, overtaking Bayern Munich and Germany legend Gerd Muller's record from 1972. Messi ended 2012 with a breathtaking 91 goals.

RECORD BREAKER

Nov 22, 2014
Scores his 252nd La Liga goal to become the highest scorer in the competion's history.

Nov 30, 2015
Messi is voted La Liga's best player for 2015. It's a record sixth time he has won the award after first picking up the trophy in 2009.

Sept 23, 2019
The Argentinian wins the Best FIFA Men's Player award for a record-breaking sixth time in his career.

Sept 18, 2018
Messi scores a hat-trick at the Nou Camp against PSV Eindhoven in the Champions League. It is the superstar's eighth treble in the competition, a new record.

Dec 8, 2018
Messi's first, he'd get a second too, against city rivals Espanyol in La Liga takes him into double figures and makes him the first player in Spanish football history to score 10 or more league goals for 13 consecutive seasons.

Jan 13, 2019
The Nou Camp hero is on target in the league in a 3-0 victory over Eibar. Messi becomes the first player to reach the 400 La Liga goals milestone.

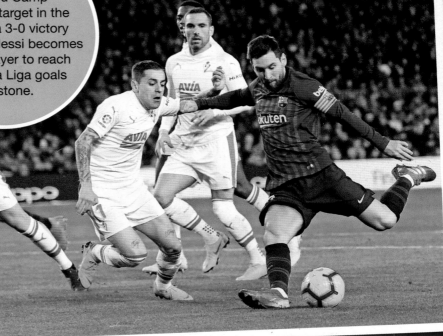

WHAT NEXT?

What does the future hold for Messi? What is there still to achieve for a man who won more individual and club medals and awards before his 30th birthday than most players achieved in their whole careers?

Although he holds the all-time La Liga scoring record – a milestone that will probably never be beaten – Messi still has plenty to play for in the rest of his career. How many more goals can he score? How many more winner's medals can he collect?

There is also his ambition to win the World Cup, to emulate what many of his Barcelona team-mates have done with Spain and what his hero Diego Maradona did with Argentina in 1986.

As for where he might play in the future, Messi has never shown any desire to leave Barcelona for another top European club. He said in 2012: "This is my home, my club. I owe everything to Barca. I'm very happy here."

His current Nou Camp contract, signed in 2017, runs out in the summer of 2021 and although it's hard to imagine the star ever playing for another club, he admits he has a long-standing desire to head back to Argentina at the end of his career.

Barça however are desperate to hang on to their greatest ever player and in the summer of 2019 it was reported that the Catalan club were ready to offer him a new deal that would keep Messi at the Nou Camp until he was 36-years-old.

"I would love to return," he said, in 2016 when asked if he would ever re-sign for his first club, Newell's Old Boys. "It is something I have kept an eye on because it was my dream as a child. Obviously my life started to change and went another way but I have no regrets. It's something I have kept an eye on. I want to play in Argentine football and Newell's, where I grew up."

As he says: "I don't think it will be until after I've retired that I'm fully aware of what I've done or what I've achieved in my career."

Spectacular goals

"I'm more concerned about being a good person than being the best footballer in the world," he said. "My hope is that when I retire that I'm remembered as a good guy."

But even if Messi does finish without breaking any more records or scoring any more spectacular goals, he has still already done more than enough to entertain millions of football fans, and then we can all bid him farewell and simply say: "Lionel Andres Messi, thanks for the memories."

Spectacular goals have given Messi's fans plenty of memories to treasure.

"This is my home, my club. I owe everything to Barça. I'm very happy here."

KNOW YOUR STUFF

Here are 20 questions to test your Messi knowledge. All of the answers can be found somewhere in the book!

1 What is Messi's middle name?

2 In which Argentinian city was Messi born?

3 Against which team did Messi score five goals in a single Champions League match in 2012?

4 Which of the following players has played alongside Messi for Argentina: Zlatan Ibrahimovic, Angel Di Maria or David Villa?

5 At what age did Messi score his first competitive goal for Barcelona in 2005?

6 Who were the same opponents in the final when Barcelona won the 2009 and 2011 Champions League titles?

7 Name Messi's first two first-team managers at Barcelona?

8 What date is Messi's birthday?

9 Messi beat the record of which former Germany striker when he scored 91 goals in 2012?

10 How many league goals did Messi score during the 2011/12 season?

11 How many La Liga goals in total did Messi score in the 2017/18 and 2018/19 seasons?

12 Against which team did Messi score his record-breaking 300th La Liga goal?

13 How many times has the Argentina superstar won the FIFA Ballon d'Or?

14 Messi made his 100th appearance in the Champions League against which Italian team?

15 Against which team did Messi score his 600th goal for Barcelona in May 2019?

16 In what year did Messi score the winning goal against Estudiantes in Abu Dhabi to earn Barcelona their first ever FIFA Club World Cup crown?

17 The striker was in brilliant form in 2015 as Barcelona lifted the Champions League trophy to complete a famous treble. Which side did they beat in the final?

18 How many FIFA World Cup finals tournaments has Messi played in?

19 How old was Messi when he became Argentina's youngest ever player in the World Cup when he came off the bench against Serbia and Montenegro in 2006?

20 In what year did Messi win an Olympic gold medal with Argentina?

It's tough work being a superstar – Messi takes a break during training with Argentina.